the thin man in our compartment
looks like charles hawtrey

the thin man in our compartment
looks like charles hawtrey
robert cochrane

Best wishes,
Robert Cochrane.

the bad press

Published in 1998 by The Bad Press,
PO Box 76, Manchester M21 8HJ

ISBN 0 9517233 7 5

1 3 5 7 9 2 4 6 8

Cover designed by Robert Cochrane.
Cover shots of Charles Hawtrey - 1950s unknown.
Author as a child - 1960s street photographer.
Author photo by Phil Chatterley.

Printed by
The Arc and Throstle Press Limited,
Nanholme Mill, Shaw Wood Road,
Todmorden, Lancs, OL14 6DA.

ACKNOWLEDGEMENTS

Morrissey for his kind permission to quote from
his song 'Miserable Lie' in 'Home On The Range'
Copyright Warner Brothers UK Ltd.
Faber and Faber for their permission to reprint
'Miss McCaw' and 'You Fell In Love'
from 'Hard Lines 3' published 1987.
Poems from pages 29-43 first appeared in
'The Perfume Of Screams' pamphlet
published 1992 by The Bad Press.
Poems from pages 44-64 appeared in
'The Thin Man In Our Compartment
Looks Like Charles Hawtrey'
published in 1988 by Civilian Editions.
Thanks to Diane Duffy, Nick Duffy,
Keith Elliot and Gary Parkinson
for their invaluable assistance.

CONTENTS

Once again for
Jonathan Sadler,
Paula Silcox
and Andrew Heard
1958 - 1993
a fellow admirer of the thin man.

Absence lessens moderate passions and intensifies great ones,
as the wind blows out a candle but fans up a fire.

Le Rochefoucauld 1613 - 1680.

In any event it shows a finer nature to be unconsciously vulgar
than to be consciously virtuous.

Truman Capote 1924 - 1984.

Nothing can ever be important or have the power to move unless
it contains within itself the possibility of death.

Madeleine Bourdouxhe 1906 - 1996.

The way sparrows fly into windows and whales beach themselves
is a journey without reason.

Donald Rawley 1957- 1998.

APART

In a neglected drawer
I found old pictures of you,
discoloured,
stuck together
like rainwept magazines.
At some forgotten party
red wine spilled
and seeped
through creaking joins
to stain neglected papers,
bits of string,
a fish blood crimson.
I gently eased apart
this evidence of you,
but your features
tore to fresh
unflatterings.

HEARTBREAK BENCH
for Sebastian Beaumont.

You call it
"Heartbreak Bench"
one of three
along the crescent
framed by your study window.
There people meet
to talk
and sometimes cry.
Perhaps the tree,
a feature absent
from the rest,
entices them,
heads bowed like spies
exchanging secrets.
It may symbolise
a sense of sanctuary,
a refuge for their tears
should their gathered grief
evoke a bitterness
or ending.

SPACE AND HICKSVILLE

When the provincial master
of our village primary
with a penchant
for turning stories
of his unwitting daughters
into religious allegories,
told the class
that London stretched
from where we sat
to beyond Belfast,
we gasped.
Towns we knew
were places you
could drive through,
ones like home,
a walking matter,
but thoughts of all
our countryside built up,
was endless,
was frightening.
This bothered me for days,
till lying in my bed
staring at the moon
to see the man,
but failing,
something greater dawned.
Space didn't stop,
neatly boxed.
It had no reason to.
It just went on forever.

POWERLESS

Jealousy
is no emotion
raised from strength,
but utter weakness,
wearing rage
as some defence.
I sensed it
gnawing in my chest,
tightening my throat;
despised this glimpse
far from my Sunday best,
my finer feelings.
I would not argue.
I could not stay.
Just left you
to your flirting,
pushed my chair
in quietly
and walked away.

A FORMAL MADNESS

My love poems seem
despite undated days
and differing tones,
a homage to
one treasured soul.
A grand illusion
as old loves combine,
instead of seeing theirs
the face on view is mine.
I wrote of others
by writing of myself,
it seems I wove
through these events
a silent madness;
the belief that repetition
of identical acts
would fulfil my hope
for a different outcome.

DON'T LOOK NOW
for Jamie Collins.

The dead go on
behind our backs
when we're not looking,
and if we sharply turn
we'd catch them out,
several steps behind
like Chinese wives.
This happens rarely,
instead they vanish down
official doorways,
merge into crowds,
or to conceal their faces,
lurk amongst
the shadows under trees.
They do not fade
transparently
like movie ghosts,
preferring freehold screens
within our minds,
to punctuate our actions,
decorate our words
with things they did,
or would have
given time.
At night they grasp
the starring roles
our dreams provide,
but rarely grant us
happy endings;
their legacies preserved

on paint and film,
ink and tape.
They do not fade away.
They grow no older.
They are merely waiting.

WANT

It was my town debut,
Saturday in a wider world,
my mother thought me
old enough at three,
but she hadn't reckoned
on the vase.
Passing the 'dear'
and now defunct
department store,
I spied a bright red
piece of glass for flowers.
Excitedly I pointed,
inwardly she guessed
if left to gaze
I'd soon lose interest.
A fixation grew
and as she wheeled me off
I cried and screamed
and no amount of soothing words
and handbag sweets,
closed my mantra of
'I want!'
The afternoon was spoilt
and town deemed
distant as before.
I didn't get the vase,
have since become more civilised,
the want transferred to human forms,
though nowadays the screams
are seldom aired.

POSTPONING

She said
'Afterwards
 the poems come.'
So ominous.
So certain.
I vowed to prove her wrong,
no urge to write once more
the laboured lines
of love fresh gone.
This time
the poetry can rot,
no need to wound myself
by gathering
such pointed words.
Yet four hours from
her stark decree
I've scribbled pages
with the beauty
only pain brings through.
I am resigned
in some way paid
like a prostitute
that needs the work.
Without you near
the poems called,
sure as the night.

KELLY'S GARDEN

He tended it
with bone gnarled fingers
drawing grace from nature
through the soil.
I'd coax with brooms
bitter black or green
plum and apple windfalls,
mindful to avoid
the honey houses
lined with threats of pain.
Hedges sheltered dahlias,
heavy headed globes
that snapped with rain,
grown for their hue,
their pollen,
they laced the evening light
with heady colours;
the honeysuckle hung
with dew from trees.
He'd give me ample bunches
of these trophies,
pink and yellow,
white,
blackcurrant dark,
every year another
startling colour,
the name carefully remembered
from the catalogue.
This dusk I passed
his former garden,

now a neat flat lawn
devoid of trees,
his labours like himself
returned to soil.
I briefly close my eyes
and all returns,
the scent,
the clacking gate,
that still faint fear of bees.

THE OTHER PAPARAZZI

I once knew a kid,
who may have grown
out of it by now,
or gone "real weird".
He'd loiter round
the clubs in town
and swoon at guys
who never glanced at him.
Unlikely to inspire adoration
he seemed doomed
to inflict it
upon others.
Once he rushed
towards us happy,
"I can't believe I've got him"
his excited words,
a camera held
like a cheap fairground prize.
I look baffled
till informed
he'd a gallery
of all his distant crushes,
startled guys
with flash-red eyes,
or faces in a crowd,
who never understood
his strange intrusions.

THE ODD GEM

You asked
if I wrote poems
for you.
In truth I have
but they're all crap.
It's nothing personal,
no reflection,
just scratching out
weak words and rhymes,
making love appear
as Barbara Cartland can ,
or the verse in greeting cards.
But like a blind man
with a camera,
there's always the odd gem.

BRITISH DENTISTRY RECALLED

You broke my heart
in several places,
one of them was Manchester
on a night busy road,
as cars eclipsed our silhouette
oblivious to the drama
going down.
I pass there daily
and remember nothing.
Yet this afternoon
and once more single,
our night returned
and left me rueful.
Since that decade
there have been other
breakages to pay for,
each fresh clatter
would eclipse the last,
but like a freeze-frame rosary
our chipped bead
has worn round,
it's batteredness familiar.
You tore us up
because our time together
passed so easily.
It took me years to see
how possible success
could terrify
such a seasoned failure.
You feared the risk of pain

so threw it all to me.
I missed your scent
and missed your smile,
once not so neat,
a tribute to the genius
of British dentistry,
and those eyes,
a gift from your mother's side
used so carelessly.

THE NUMBERS GAME
for Eleanor, 1896-1996.

She went with little fuss,
went without saying.
A brief notice
in the local rag,
a tiny funeral the result
of living into remnancy,
downstairs
behind old windows.
A few months more
and there'd have been
a telegram,
and the sort of frenzy
living out a century
entails.
'Oldest Resident In Town'
she would have loathed,
for everyone
then knew her age,
her gripe at ninety.
She lived beyond outings,
beyond pleasure,
housebound from all
she'd once enjoyed
and then endured.
I saw her house,
it's curtains met,
the door in need of paint,
in death like life
if uninformed,
I'd think
she was still there.

A POEM FOR MITRA SAGHARZADEH

Now we cannot meet
by matinee suggested means;
your last detail
a card so censored
it was senseless.
I hate to think you
trapped in black,
that beauty starkly veiled
in your home country.
I conjure an escape
under darkness of some night,
the Persian moon discreetly
failed to shine,
as you fled holy men
who loathed the secular
and any who should act
against their line.
When you'd turn heads
it thrilled me,
a teenage kick
to smile at now,
but rue I creased
your party dress
the night my armour fell,
though I never cried upon
a finer shoulder.
On our last encounter
before Trafalgar's lions
below a Christmas sky,

I said you were beautiful.
You frowned
and called me silly,
the evidence,
imagined flaws
from details in your mirror.
A summer on
I wrote your name
along an Irish shore,
sorry you would never
walk along it,
watching as the waves
dispelled that sweetheart notion.
I have no photographs,
your voice the merest cliché.

A VERY NICE WAY TO GO

Two old girls
hobble down the churchyard
talking of another's passing on.
'She'd been to the hairdressers
that very morning.
Came home,
sat down with a cuppa
and died.
Oh it was.
Indeed it was
a very nice way to go.'
Providing I wasn't
in bed with someone
at the time,
to go in my sleep
always seemed
the desired line.
Recently
my thoughts have changed.
I'd like to know
it was happening
if it were a tranquil
deathbed scene.
That last experience,
a memory lost
by dying through it.
Birth ever unremembered
death becomes the same.

A PREFERENCE FOR MEMORY

Passion,
pressing sweetness
from ripening lips,
anxiously confessing
love through fingertips.
Such things we had,
but more than most,
ours was a tryst
stamped of its time.
No film exists
of running from the rain,
our laughter at a misplaced phrase;
of looks that warmed
the heart for days.
No letters ribbon-bound,
no postcards scrawled
with afterwords,
for more than most
we had a love
used up like fuel.
I have a video,
you before
the crossings of our lives,
a version in another's gaze,
which gathers dust
since all went down.
I remember you
as better looking,
more geared for living,
in the way remembered songs
sound better too.

ON SOMETHING

You said
'There's something
 not quite right about
 the girl in the sweet shop'.
I disagreed.
'She cheers me up'
but you maintained
'Nobody can be
 that happy all the time
 unless they're on something'.
I got your drift
though it didn't quite appeal,
some must incline to smile
with a lilt in their voice,
like the girl in sweetshop
who always cheers me.
Otherwise
I wouldn't notice her,
and you wouldn't know
which girl I meant.
But then again
maybe she is
'on something'.

THE ALTAR OF LIFE

The scene
of crumpled sheets
and rumpled thoughts,
cold sickly sweats
or salt-sweet ones,
the alchemy of love.
Conceived and born
and borne away
on this altar of life,
we rest there
after bitter days,
a haven of peace,
a cave from storms.
Sleep,
warmed by
expensive weaves
or yesterday's papers,
like death falls
equal upon all.
With our final exit,
the bed,
that place of nightmares
and of dreams,
is made by others.

SUNDIAL BANK

Where I lived once
exists no more.
Displaced
upon its mound
the sundial base,
a headstone
in pastiche of burial.
Now memory,
a sunlit hall,
stained glass shadows
glancing dullish lino,
the tree which scraped
my window eerily
in streetlit nights of rain.
Burnt years after
my departure,
decorating I had done
still visible
through damp and drizzle.
The thriftiness of landlords.
No shell
for recognition left,
the name upon its pillars,
slumped sentries to 'Victoriana',
the final marks of trouble,
pain and laughter
in my rented rooms,
faded and distant
like a childhood scar.

BETWEEN THE SHEETS

In his fantasy
perhaps they are
in love with him,
the kind of women
he has dreamt of,
caring and attentive
to his needs.
As he becomes
the masterful lover,
a lean limbed male
of classic mode.
This is unlikely,
his excitement
more a schoolboy's
hurried fumbling.
He bravely wobbles
on two sticks,
a built up boot
dragged towards the counter,
clutching
sealed polythene delights,
naked girls he'd never view,
unless between such sheets.

ORIGIN OF THE CLICHÉS

They were not always
truth worn bare,
grasped without experience
in thoughtless repetition,
broken clocks,
twice right each day,
they even now retain
a certain wisdom.
A cliché is
the boring truth
lazily recited,
as routines of existence
make each generation learn
things the past
had come to know.
Much is doomed
to cliché,
as in origin
and culmination,
we become them.

THE POINT
for Keith Haring

When illness had
deprived him
the holding of a pencil,
he took another's hand
and moved it through the air,
creating in that unity
lines he could no longer
draw alone.
In that act,
the gesture lost
as it was made,
the essence lies
to all our making marks.
Futility
stole no meaning from
his drawing into space,
but took him to the point
suspended in the moment,
as music does that stirs
fulfilment beyond being;
living neither
in the present
or the future.

BEFORE NOW

Maintaining
happy memories
requires stealth,
faith against the changes
in our days,
the blasphemies of life.
Soiled
by subsequent events,
we are incapable
of disentangling
the origin and middle
from the end.
They should survive
when reassessed,
but the present,
is a vantage point
which colours every vision,
mocking or revering
our memories
before now.

TEN YEARS AFTER

A mournful song
brought to mind
those winter's with you,
to under-score your absence.
For warmth
I'd wear your coat
in that grand
- but freezing place,
thinking such apparel
the most romantic symbol.
We threw stones
on a frozen pond,
a tuned percussion in the ice,
as laughter and white breath
embossed such simple fun.
The broken guttering
thawed across a barren tree,
making it as those
in 'Ice Queen' stories.
I marvelled at your face,
would look long and shamelessly,
which drew rightful irritation
across such even features.
All that returned
listening to a song
unwritten in those days,
though with the window's frost,
the ice on the tree
and the pond,
we are gone.

SAD BIOLOGY

We replace
humility with disgust,
twist intimacy
to derision.
Organs of creation
are labels for disdain,
the rituals of conception
much the same.
By language
we demean
our spark to being,
deride generic needs
with base retorts.
In mocking the profound
we betray self-loathing
as we curse
what we most crave,
and shudder
at the mention
of the stuff
that made us.

DESIRE

Desire stems
from primal themes
surging for release
in order to maintain
our breed on earth,
but has evolved beyond
such instincts.
Monogamy unquestioned
and promiscuous extremes
are neither
happily secure
nor wantonly perverse,
but mere confessions to
a nagging sense of loneliness.
decidedly humane.
by nature flawed.
that brave admission
could render us more loveable
Instead we erect walls.
evolve games from debris
and pretend,
foxing love with desire,
thought with emotion,
Though we cannot live
one without the other,
this imbalance of alchemies
sparks petrol in emotion
and reservoirs of intellect
cannot save us
from the flames.

A BOOK OF REVELATIONS

Sorted
as I had
a dead man's words,
familiar to the point
of blind contempt,
my poems became
an exercise in form,
dead skin laid-out.
In print
the pain of buried days
revived to claim their source.
Mouthing every word
as an intruder
on a diary,
I cringed at finished, truths.
Cringed again
at my reflection
held within a reader's eye,
and wished them words
of any hand
but mine.

SECONDARY EDUCATION

We learn life's lesson
in reverse.
Ruby expectations hide
the grails of love
and trust
and friends,
are mostly myths.
If lucky
we may never see
the mirage in such hope,
though usually we curse
that failure to
prepare us
for the worst,
and not the rare occasions
when dreams don't burst.

THE COMMON LOVE OF PEPE

In the fifties
for your birthday
your mother went to buy a bear,
but there being none that day
she bought a monkey.
Pepe, she said
was like a child,
a found 'dummy'
ever in his mouth,
undressed himself
in winter weather,
so was chained.
He hated that,
ate his tale in boredom
like parrots plucking out
their feathers within cages.
Two years on,
aware of this
in cruel kindness,
she returned him,
 'dummy' still in place,
to the pet shop.
The owner had a buyer
with a large garden
who wanted a monkey,
even one with half a tail.
"He howled," she said,
howled in such distress
as she walked down the street,
those screams still haunt her.

Her story
echoed my reply
as you declared
"Love isn't real.
 We make it up."
I felt it did
though not the way
we most expect,
could only add
 "We see it best in animals.
 Instinctive.
 Unspoilt by reason."
If something you desire
holds the power of pain,
your feelings have the answer.
Though I never heard
Pepe and his screaming,
as a child lost in Woolworth's,
or a lover scorned,
I know their meaning.

WISDOM OF SOAP

Watching standard love
slide to standard pain,
I wondered why we view
such scenes,
again and then again,
in pale or garish
imitations of the real.
'Just like life'
an accolade,
a craved for confirmation
to smooth the past,
console our future.
Most lives and loves,
numbingly the same.

IGNORANCE WAS THIS

At the checkout
she realised
as the assistant
lifted them,
the apples in her basket
were South African.
She tactfully explained
'I never buy
 anything from there.'
The woman nodded
understandingly
'I don't blame you love.
 Who'd want them anyway
after all those
big black hands
have been over them?'

ACCIDENTS WILL HAPPEN

Seated in sunshine
by the fete marquee,
an old lady
kind faced,
uneasy on her feet.
asked if we'd mind her bag
and 'Thank-You'
stiffly waddled away.
Minutes later,
resembling an aged child
clutching a cornet,
she tried to squeeze
between chairs
and fell,
face into ice-cream.
A motherly gaggle
with matronly awkwardness
hoisted her upright,
the blue hat slipped
from crowning
vanilla splattered features,
farcing her disgrace.
They wiped her features
with scented handbag hankies,
left her in the shade
to recover from indignity.
She soon was chatting again,
buying little china plates
with cats on.

THE THIN MAN

The thin man
in our compartment
looks like Charles Hawtrey,
in a baggy black suit,
from round horn rims
he views
the underside of England.
No-one is waving to us,
only dead houses roll by
as we shunt towards
our rainy destination.
He ignores well
as you loudly exclaim
feeling old,
since the present
and the past
have grown inseparable.
Your gestures are charming.
a beauty to the eye.
In a life
of almosts and not quites,
you almost killed yourself last night;
the self-made martyr failed
to hammer in that final nail.
Past our silent companion
you chance a glance
to the industrial view,
in the tunnel he catches
our reflections on dark glass,
and quickly looks away.

Despite your seriousness
I half imagine a bra-clad
Barbara Windsor to shriek in,
pursued by a cackling Sid James
and an indignant Kenneth Williams.
hands raised in horror.
But your 'Carry-On' isn't funny.
and the thin man
in our compartment
only looks like Charles Hawtrey.

THORN FARM
for Jonathan Sadler.

Hector used to sit and watch,
a silent listener to our conversation.
He sees nothing now
and hears less,
but where he senses us
he looks unblinkingly
with misted eyes.
The rose that overhangs
the blue porch door
scents every breath
and the sun slowly sinks
behind the thatch,
as it has more evenings
than we will ever know.
Departure beckons,
Hector may not live to leave.
his blindness could not adjust
to walls and corners
unfamiliar
from his sighted times.
To this winding place
of little rooms.
added at the need or whim
of forgotten generations,
time seems belied,
and grants scant preference
to the living.
The monks have gone.
their order lost,
the priest hole shelters

pigeons more than haunted scribes,
but the lodger,
ex-army,
lay preacher,
religious teacher at a local school,
who spends his evenings
writing sermons in his room,
maintains this old tradition.
As we cross the smoothness
of the Jacobean tiles.
beneath the buckled ceiling
with it's decorated beams.
a sense of passing
and past time
ran a shiver on my spine.
People have lived here
for twelve hundred years,
and when successors
speculate as we,
of all the souls
who've lived and cried
within these many walls,
they will not know of these lines,
or that Hector
was an old terrier
aged 17.

ONCE AND FOR ALL

Once
he must have
rough-housed with his friends,
drank a little much,
ran laughing in the sun
for no good reason.
Once
he may have
partied after dark,
met girls in the park,
made love to some
and loved a few.
Ambition
might have led him,
may still stir
regret for things
unconquered then
and now forever.
Once
he could walk tall,
talk into the quiet hours,
looking forward with
youth's wasteful span.
Now he leans
out of breath and old
upon his walking frame,
waiting for a break
in evening traffic.

MISS McCAW
1910 - 1983

Sam was big hats
and gaudy scarves,
long billowing skirts,
fox furs,
heavy coats and cardigans.
A fashion refugee of the 1940s.
In his teens
the farmer's daughter
dressed him for fun
the farm-boy
in her things.
He refused
to be anything else.
When laughter
and cold reason failed,
he was not put away,
in country eyes
he did no harm,
so was let be.
They added
an old term to his name,
from then on he became
'Sam Mary Ann'.
The war years
meant dances in local halls,
powder caked
betraying stubble shadows,
she'd retouch that curious face,
observing huskily
in failed feminine tones

'There's a lot of Big Yankees here tonight!'
Men danced her for fun,
grinning past those shoulders
to their pals.
One let his hands
wander towards the truth,
a punch sprawled him
down the chair-edged wall.
In the chemist's
she'd request
as if in passing
'Some razor blades
 for my next-door neighbour.'
Male hands holding gloves,
thick ankles squeezed
into fine shoes,
her hat at a jaunty angle
and the faithful old bicycle
wall-leant outside.
When called to give evidence,
she dressed in her finest.
The unwarned judge
angrily assumed contempt
before tact and explanation
intervened.
In hospital
she raised hell
in the men's ward.
They had to understand.
She was Miss McCaw!
The eventual compromise
a room of her own.
We used to wolf whistle

and shout 'Hi Ya Sam!'
kissing the windows
of our school bus.
She'd shake her fist
unladyfully and glower.
Some risked
bravado in the street
but Sam gave chase
and if successful
dispersed her callers
with bruised ears.
In town
she caused no stir
and stirred no causes.
Everyone said hello
as they do in Ireland
and Sam said the same
on her way to shop
or chat and tea
with some of her old lady friends.
She never met one like herself,
nor spoke of the situation,
that would have betrayed
her act of years,
in gladrags with handbags
passed along or bought
from jumble sales.
Yet in death
they dressed her in
a black suit and a tie
and combed back her hair.
A male discretion of embalmer's rouge,
the sole concession

to a lifetime spent
in woman's ways,
or a perception of them.
She was betrayed,
but only briefly.
A headstone to 'S. McCaw'
restored her sense
of mystery.

HOME ON THE RANGE

I sense sometimes
she's here,
disapproving of my presence
and the present.
Absent of her things
these generous rooms
shelter more with less,
'Sundial Bank'
its namesake now
a sandstone base.
Her ghostly skirts
sweep uncarpeted stairs,
whilst the garden
and its weeds
have never known such peace.
The street is more untidy
in autumnal litter,
as cars crawl kerbs
for 'short-time' favours,
a sad testament
to its time and signs.
'Derwent Place'
a fading name from
sloped and weathered pillars,
its rubble overgrown
like ancient graves.
Perhaps,
she and he
walk in despair
at disrepair,

their unheard children
horrified
by the unemployed hairdresser
with the taloness nails,
her four cats
of no fixed pedigree,
and the girl shorn
beneath the blue beret.
Like dogs these houses
have had their day,
the once posh outskirt
an inner-city area.
In evenings
lashed by rain.
words of one
who fled this foul domain,
confirm my passing sadness.
'What do we get for our trouble and pain?
 Just a rented room in Whalley Range.'

EVERYDAY GHOSTS

In these early hours
the piano's sound
slips through many rooms
and soothes
as the storm brews.
I am writing in your coat,
the first to come to hand
since the chill
sought out my bones
and I drew cold
from the stone floor.
The old settle creaks
to my every move,
not forgotten to working worms
it might have proved
quite valuable.
You have exhausted
your out of tune recital
on nail-bitten
and discoloured keys,
the toll of damp upon
that rickety upright.
We are just as volatile,
our collective years
show faces with an age,
in this poor light
much older than ourselves.
You brought her here.
a grown ghost,
as winter bore its toll

upon a fading year.
She saw recognition
in their second glances
understood it in their voices,
but when she viewed the photograph
that hangs before the stairs,
saw it for herself
and wondered
without answer.

CONVERSATION WITH THE FLY MAN

The church bell softly rang
like an old clock
in a nearby room.
Much accustomed by the years
he leant across the table
with its vintage dust of crumbs
and spoke like some old actor
treading lines.
'I talked with him
  for hours when he died.
  In that cold room
  piled up with junk and jumble,
  I told his corpse the things
  I couldn't tell a soul.
  They do not call it
  lunacy for nothing'
His old eyes darkened
with this pearl.
'At full moon
  he became a stranger
  who ranted to the walls
  his deeper thoughts.
  Madness may be that,
  it may be more.
  The locals claim I'm so,
  as though the sane can know.
  They call me 'The Fly Man'
  for in the park or square
  I let all insects
  crawl upon my face,

even those who sting
will not
if you leave them
to their wandering.
For unlike they!'
His craggy finger cast
an aged wave of irritation
to the window none were passing.
'I cannot kill.
I am but a greater insect
on a greater face.'
His voice of rust
ground silent
in his figuring of figments,
till an earlier thread
broke quiet of his making.
'You see
I understood his strangeness.
When you understand
words contradict,
blatant things used uselessly
in statement or question.'
He glanced about the fusty den.
a smile along his thin dark lips
and bore a sigh betraying
both worldliness and pain.
'Though he knew
all this and more.
I wish I could have told him
while he breathed.'

YOU FELL IN LOVE
for Chrissie.

You fell in love
age 8
with a dustman
and his bright smile.
You used to skate
up and down,
down and up,
swooning at him
on his rounds.
After all
the leaning
and the looking,
you courageously confessed.
He took
his teeth out
and said
'You can have it'.

CLARE PARK
28th December 1985

The final time
a porter closed these gates
now held by twisted wire,
is no clear memory,
his lodge encroached by ivy,
doorless, roofless,
without windows.
No gravel left to rake,
the drive is mud
much marked by sheep
that flee before us
towards the house,
a larger ruin.
Castellated from country plain,
in true Victorian grossness
this walled domain
seems a fortress
in some forgotten fable.
The tower with the spiral stairs
is rife for clinking swords
and straining bows,
though in its present state
it would appear
the siege is over.
Curtains hang
like rotten shrouds
at splintered panes,
doors cracked and ceilings
ready to descend the darkness
where the floor once was.

There is a glory here
amidst the cold
of glories flown.
Some shadows distant
of the house,
within the sloping earth,
lies an ex-incumbent of its walls.
He died in 1923,
an accident along the cliffs
and as requested in his wishes
was laid to rest
between the bodies
of his finest racing steeds.
An iron-cast surround
is their sole saviour
from the nibbling flock,
some of whom like he
fell to their deaths
in last year's storm.
Now for sale,
a crumbled residence
with a perilous view,
a grave as evidence
and added curio of one
who in old splendid days
looking from where windows were,
would not in wildest flights
have thought
it all would end
as this.

DANDELIONS

As a child
I thought
dandelions beautiful,
picked them by the armful,
stirring smiles in adults
and those my age
playing at maturity.
Though tutted at
and teased,
I continued my passion
undeterred.
They were colourful,
nice to touch
and free.
Even now
I sneak a bunch
into the living room,
aware I must maintain
their honesty
in more worldly avenues.